from
Taskmasters
to
Tambourines

an exodus narrative to spiritual freedom

John Pace

Author: John Pace

Date Published: March 1, 2018

ISBN: 978-0-9986221-2-5

Publisher: Crimson House Ministries

Copyright © Crimson Houses Ministries 2018

© 2018 Crimson Houses Ministries. All rights reserved. This material may not be reproduced, displayed, modified or distributed without the prior and express written permission of the copyright holder.

Scripture quotations taken from the New American Standard Bible® (NASB), Copyright © 1960, 1962, 1963, 1968, 1971, 1972, 1973, 1975, 1977, 1995 by The Lockman Foundation Used by permission. www.Lockman.org

All enquiries via www.crimsonhouseministries.org

Contents

Preface 5
Chapter One 11
Chapter Two 15
Chapter Three 19
Chapter Four 25
Chapter Five 29
Chapter Six 33
Chapter Seven 37
Chapter Eight 41
Chapter Nine 47
Chapter Ten 49
Chapter Eleven 55
Chapter Twelve 57
Chapter Thirteen 61
Chapter Fourteen 65
Chapter Fifteen 69
Chapter Sixteen 73
Chapter Seventeen 79
About the Author 85

Preface

Taskmasters to Tambourines had been an inspiration for nearly ten years, but the key to that unction came just a few short months ago in a conversation with my wife of 36 years.

Diane, a gifted intercessor, shared with me how in her devotion the Spirit revealed to her a different side in the Exodus story. It was a new facet for me on the diamond that is Scripture. Upon hearing it, the empowering unction for this book grabbed my spirit.

She shared how Moses was a type of our spiritual man and Israel a type of our natural man, which now makes Exodus a story of our personal battle between the two for deliverance. It was the key in unlocking the unction for this narrative.

How thankful I am for a wife who *helped* me *meet* the fullness of a decade-old inspiration.

Exodus 3-15 is the outline for *Taskmasters to Tambourines* through the matrix of the 'types' written above. I sincerely hope you find this story as inspiring to you as it was for me in its writing.

John Pace
February 2018

So if the Son makes you free, you will be free indeed.
John 8:36

preparation

"…Before Abraham was…I AM."

John 8:58

Chapter One

Something happened to me today as I walked in that spiritually arid place in my life. You may know of a place like that too; seems like everyone does. It's where I leave my lush walk in the Spirit and travel in the dryness of my flesh. It's where I serve the taskmaster rather than the Master. It is a place of fruitless aggravation; and yes, I hate that place—just like you do. But I can't escape it. It's been traversed for years—seems like forty or so, but that's hard to say. Having wandered around in its dryness so long, I am resigned to the fact that I will never leave. I have conceded that, in this particularly personal place, my history has forever determined my future.

But as I said, something happened to me today. I must have walked this path a thousand times and never saw it...or maybe God, in His grace, wanted my attention; maybe in His mercy, He had heard my parched and whispered desire to leave this dry and thirsty land. It was there in my daily routine, practiced comfortably for decades now, that I was abruptly interrupted. I was arrested by a sight I have never seen: a bush on fire, yet consumed not. It was a fire unlike any other, for the flame I witnessed on the outside had ignited an inner burning that caused me to draw closer to see just what was before me. Then, in that nearness deep inside my spirit, the truly indescribable fire spoke to me.

Speaking my name, He stopped me in my tracks. It is amazing how you can stop in the deepness of your spirit while never moving an inch on your feet. But I did. I stopped at His powerful, yet compassionate, command to go no further. His holiness would not be breached by anything man-made. I had gone as far as I could go on my own; yet, I was not on my own. I had not initiated this journey. He had, by starting that fire that burned within me. But I did take notice. I did turn and look. You see, there are some things we must do, but even in that work He is the initiator.

He, the God of my fathers, said He had heard my cry. He had heard from His heavenly dwelling my cry to be delivered of my taskmaster and expelled from the desert land he rules. God said He would come down and deliver; He would deliver me from the power of my enslaver. Oh, it had been so long, for so long I had cried to be free…and now He said He had heard! His words, so empowered by His holiness, brought hope to my being, tears to my eyes, and chagrin to my soul. There, in my sinful embarrassment, in my loss-of-face, I hid my face from the very One who loved me more than I loved myself; the One who loved me more than I loved my own fruitless ways that I had chosen over Him—time, after time, after time.

Chapter Two

"I AM that I AM," God said to my spirit man.

"But," I wondered, "who am I that God would speak to me? Who am I, that the God of the heavens would come down and deliver me from my bondage?"

He continued, "You have known Me as an historic God, the one of your fathers, but I AM not just a God of yesterday…I AM ever-present. Though I AM the same yesterday, today, and forever, I have no yesterday or today, for I AM forever—I AM both before forever and forever after and everything in-between. I AM."

The magnitude of such a description added to the shame of my slavery. "Who am I to be delivered? I am destined to bondage, just like my father and his father as well. You were their God, and in the same way, You are mine too. I am a nomad hiding this sinful area of my life in this desert wilderness. Yes, I find an occasional oasis of hope and a temporary reprieve from my sinful plight, but I never leave this outback. I am, and I always will be, in this wilderness. In fact, I am just the lead-follower in a sinful flock; I am slow of speech and I am..." I replied in degenerating succession.

"No, I AM," thundered His interruption of my self-belittlement. "And you will see the extent of that I AM." He then displayed before my spiritual eyes His omnipotence and omniscience in renewing the leper-like sin of my hand and revealing the fear in my heart.

"You will be delivered, and you will be free to worship me in this area of your life; and it will be without any sandy, gritty residue in your being," He said.

"Your adversary will fight not wanting to let you go, but I will battle for you; I will defeat every obstacle and every excuse that has kept you in bondage.

You will be set free because I AM with you," concluded the Omnipresent.

For the first time in a very, very long time, I sensed a new hope for a release from this bondage I'm in. For the first time in a long time, I had a rock to stand on rather than shifting sand. It was because God revealed into my spirit the footing for acquittal: my

"I am" must become His "I AM." The many failed attempts of, "today, I am going to be delivered" now finally concludes with "I am free because 'I AM!'"

My liberation won't be effortless; yet, it won't be arduous either...because faith never is. Oh, and it won't be instantaneous, but a journey filled with faith-trying delays. However, at the end of the pilgrimage it *will still be* miraculous.

Chapter Three

"So," I mused uneasily, drawing out the word as long as my breath would allow. "My deliverance journey begins with me going backwards; I must return to the very place that I am hiding from," I restated inwardly the directions given me.

Knowing my thoughts, He said, "Yes, and you will face the very one who owns your slavery."

Facing my sin's owner and addressing any consequence of my iniquities are some main reasons I'm living in the desert. It's easier to live in hiding, though I hate it, than to face the reality of my sin. But I must face it, I must not fear the return to that place of my collapse and, most importantly, I must not be afraid to look at myself in the process. I must try again to be free.

But this time it's different. All my thoughts, dreams, and failed attempts for living in total liberty the life God had for me may really transpire—it may literally happen. My freedom could actually leave the imaginary and become a reality. All because I am not alone: the I AM is with me!

…And so is my family.

My father-in-law said go; my spouse and children are traveling with me. This time really is different. I am not seeking freedom in seclusion, buried in the sand, with the hopes of attending a family reunion in personal triumph all clean and free; rather, I am openly moving from the backside of the desert to camp in God's land of freedom. And my family is sojourning with me.

But my sin nearly cost us an unbelievable price early in our journey.

It wasn't the sin that prompted my seclusion which nearly cost the life of my child. Rather, it was the sin of omission, which followed that far-reaching sin of commission, that almost killed him. I had failed in keeping the covenant of my God. In the selfishness of my sin, I had never shared the ordinances commanded to my fathers by the God of my fathers, who is now with me.

Truthfully, I was so self-absorbed in my sin, with the Lord's ordinances so distant from my mind, that my spouse had to intercede for the life of our loved one in that trying moment as we camped early on in our return. (In fact, I am oblivious as to the number of times it may have been done before as I wandered in my wilderness). It was this intercession, however, that both secured our journey and anchored me with understanding. I absolutely can't go forward to freedom by forgetting the words of my God; it is His truth that will set me free.

There is no freedom in the journey alone or else I would always be wandering from journey to journey. The genuine journey to freedom will lead me to that place where His word transforms my "I am" to the "I AM" in my life.

Thus, my journey began by returning: Returning to the place I feared, returning to the knowledge of His word, and returning to the practice of His life-giving decrees.

process

"I AM the light of the world...."

John 8:12

Chapter Four

I'm coming home.

I survived my sins—the one that drove me to the desert and the other that stopped me on my journey back. In returning to the place of my failure I was received with open arms. No fear, no apprehension, no condemnation, just a familial embrace at the outer edge of my trek home. There, on the Mount of God, that place high above the trials of life where His love reigns completely, my brother met me. My brother, whom I haven't seen in years since my sudden departure, welcomed me with a kiss.

I shared with him all that I AM had put in my spirit; and he had something to share too. God had prompted him to meet me as I came home. God had spoken to my brother to welcome me as I came near. The Omniscient knew I would be here, He knew that even with all my failures I would be here, right now, embraced by my brother.

My mind raced back to when I made I AM angry as He spoke with me regarding my return. I remember having continued my personal objections as to why I couldn't be a part of any deliverance. I had spoken it with such stubbornness that I AM was incensed. In that battle of words, He offered my brother as help. I didn't think much of it then. I was too stiff-necked to think past the immediate moment. But now, in the presence of love—both my brother's and I AM's—it all came back…and I felt so humbled.

In that humbling I realized that I AM, in His great love for me, could have done so many other things than give me the help of a brother. He could have dismissed me then and there, allowing me to 'win' the argument and lose my life. He could have left me alone, let me try to return on my own strength and fail like so many times before. He could have never approached me at all. But in I AM's endless love and mercy, He stayed with me and prepared a brother to help.

My brother now stood with me; not by his own accord, but by the design of I AM. Together we recognized and agreed that this time was the right time to be delivered. It was in that revelation that my entire being—body, soul, and spirit—meshed as one with the thought of being free. Then, in that moment of unveiling, I did something I had not done in such a long time. Together with my brother, and in unspeakable thankfulness to our God, I bowed my head in worship.

Chapter Five

Today is the day I'm set free. All I must do is confront the owner of my sin. I must challenge the one who knows my weakness and hits me when I'm down, and with each punch takes me even deeper into my personal abyss. But I'm better prepared this time. In fact, more prepared than I have ever been before: The I AM is with me, my family is with me, and my brother is with me. I am ready to face the test and leave with a victory.

Armed by my meeting with I AM, I challenged the tempter—the owner of my sin—to let me go to worship my God in total freedom. I had expected a quick response in the affirmative. After all, I had been obedient up to now. Surely the chief taskmaster would simply say, "Go," and out I would prance in triumphant celebration.

But my planned victorious strut quickly became a subservient slog as the tempter's blows landed one after another.

"I do not know the Lord," said the father of lies, "And I will not let you go."

"But He, the I AM, met with me," I responded, trying to be as verbally strong with the tempter in my argument as I was with I AM several days before.

"I will not let you go," he repeated, as this third blow began to take its toll on me.

And then came the knockout punch: "Your burden will be doubled," he countered, "And it will take twice as much work to resist it now; it will be doubly hard to think about freedom because you will spend all your time working in, or around, your sin. No need to think about being free or to plan to worship in liberty from now on. You are going nowhere but deeper into bondage."

How could this be? as the thought of heavier bondage rattled through my being. *How could this be; I've done everything I AM said and I'm still not free! Why did you even send me back here? I am worse off now than before! My life-seeking confrontation has put a death-sword in the hand of the tempter,* I cried in both aggravation and desperation. *It is better that I would have never come to this place,* I concluded in the pain of my short-sightedness.

But lost to me in this apparent defeat by the tempter was a new action I failed to see. Up until now any failure would send me willingly back to the short-lived solace of my iniquity; even in the slightest setback I would lose myself in the brief pleasure of sin for a season. However this time it didn't happen. This loss didn't return me to my sinful habit and its resulting despair, but this "loss" directed me back to the I AM and the hope He inspires. Rather than alienating myself further from my deliverance as I had done so many times in the past, I had, unknowingly, in my lament to God, taken one step closer to being free. For even squatting in the corner of complaint, I was in a place He could lead me on.

And that's just what I AM did. He was going to advance me on my journey, not through any volition of my own, but simply by reminding me of just who He is.

Chapter Six

I AM speaks through centuries like they were mere seconds.

He reminded me of His promise to my fathers and their fathers too. Not just the promise alone, but His remembrance of that covenant as well. Generations may have come and gone, but He is still the same; His word just as binding now as it was hundreds of years ago. He also shared how He was 'God Almighty' to them. For generations He was *El Shaddai*—God, the One of the mountain with invincible strength and power. But then He said something which rebounded throughout my spirit and still eluded capture: "But by My name, LORD, I did not make Myself known to them."

There, as I crouched in despair with my head between my knees, wondering why the Almighty One wasn't almighty or else I would be free, I AM tried to encourage me. First through the revelation from El Shaddai to Yahweh; that is, from knowing that God is almighty to *knowing* I AM's power personally. Yes, there is a difference between knowing and *knowing*. Then I AM shared how He would show me His power in my deliverance. He reiterated all that He had done in the past and then what His plans were for *my* future. Seven times He perfectly said, "I will" do this for me. Seven times. *Seven times.*

I could count the times of I AM's 'I will' and hear the revelation that Yahweh is for me, but its truth was yet to be embraced. For while I AM was ministering to my spirit, my flesh was screaming louder. My initial confrontation with the chief taskmaster only resulted in greater attacks through an environment of heavier bondage. How could I overcome that? I had failed so many times before without this new barrage. And then there is my inadequacy, that one thing I argued with I AM about in the desert, that one thing that made Him angry with me—if only for a moment.

Why do I constantly bring it up? I AM knows me better than I know myself; yet, I consistently use my weakness as the excuse for my bondage. I AM says that weakness doesn't matter, for His strength can overcome it, but I'm not there yet. Even though I have walked a great distance for my freedom, even though I AM has spoken to me clearly, I am still not there yet.

Yet I was there for a brief season. I was there before I became a fugitive from faith. I was in that place of His strength when I met my brother and spoke all I AM had shared with me; we even went to confront my taskmaster in that short-lived strength. I remember that place where I was just a short time ago. It was the outer edge of home, the Mount of God, that place high of faith above the trials of life, where His love reigns completely and where fear, and excuse, and inadequacies are cast out.

It was then, in that remembrance, the revelation began to take root, that move from knowing the Almighty to experiencing the Almighty *in* me. The battle I am in is to let I AM in the battle. When I leave the edge of home—the place of Presence—and let my eyes see the natural without the faith of the high-place Presence, I succumb to the taskmaster below. On my own I cannot combat the owner of my sin, but I AM can…and I AM will…and I AM was going to show me.

Chapter Seven

For the next nine months or so, I AM displayed His holy power by opening my eyes to the spiritual life that He is. He methodically revealed Himself as God to so many life spheres, areas where I had erected idols but areas where He wanted to be Lord of all. He completely, some 10 times, affirmed His omnipotence over my many false-gods; yet, at the same time unveiled the single support of each. That support was pride; pride was the bedrock of my every idol.

Pride certainly can be an obvious practice. Like when the chief taskmaster hesitated not in submitting to my initial encounter for freedom. He cited his ignorance of my God as reason. But pride can also be like an elusive eidolon. It can subtly influence and then sink back into the depths of its darkness. How else could you describe my arguing with I AM. Did I really believe I could know better than the Omniscient? But I did, I reminded I AM of my insufficiency as *my reason* for bondage. I pridefully, though I wouldn't have thought it at the time, challenged I AM, not once but twice.

But pride's plague was going to be treated in me. It was a treatment that would lead me to my freedom.

My remedy began with water. I AM showed me that He is the living water and all other has the bloody stench of death. Pride will tell me I can drink from any of the world's fountains I would like, any and all could quench my thirst, but only the water that is I AM keeps me from thirsting again.

Lust was the next idol I AM addressed. He showed me it is never fulfilled, but simply jumps, frog-like, from one thing to another. In that, I AM also defined the fundamental difference between lust and love: lust is *selfish* whereas love is *selfless*. Pride says I can control my lust and that love *is* all about me; however, I AM exposed that lie. The truth is I am powerless to overcome lust for only I AM cannot fall to that temptation, and that love lays down its life for another.

By using tiny insects—lice—I AM revealed how the chief taskmaster uses these minuscule parasites to covertly deceive his slaves to believe life is found in creation rather than the Creator.

The taskmaster uses pride to say my wisdom is supreme, and in that faulty wisdom, worship what I wish and live in the bondage of that belief. But I AM showed me that a fool says in his heart there is no God.

Following the treatment of these first three idols, I AM made a change in my restorative regiment. By breaking my pride that built up this worldly triune, I learned the need to truly serve Him with my whole being. I must in body, soul, and spirit let I AM be my Master: in body, by drinking the living water; in soul, by offering selfless love: and in spirit, by worshiping the Creator. It was then, after the fundamental revelation of a spiritual life, I AM made an adjustment to my remedy. Yes, there are still other idols to deal with and their accompanying pride, but a change was made—a distinction, if you will. And He used a maggot that would fly to show me.

Chapter Eight

As flies swarmed, buzzed, and fastened themselves to the natural eyes of worldly ones, I AM kept them from bothering me—completely. No swarms required me to swat them away, there was no annoying buzzing to hear and none ever came close to my eyes. It was then that I saw just what I AM desired of me: a life separated from the world. Just as He distinguished the flies' prey between His people and the taskmaster's, I AM wants me set apart from the world. He wants me to come out from among them and be that separated one unto Him.

I AM then showed me the areas in my life that needed to be given to Him, totally, so I could live this separated life. He is to be the only God of my property, my body, my provision, and my protection. Pride will want to build bigger barns, treat my body as I wish, take me into a love of material things, and be my own defender. But my foundation to those idols must be razed.

In their place must be the fear of I AM more than the fear of man; treating my body as His temple; having no anxiety for today, for the day is sufficient of itself—He will take care of it to my contentment; and letting Him fight my battles.

Oh, how I need to let Him fight my battle for me. I have fought this bondage on my own for so long, and failed, that this idol must be as vast as the worldly supply cities built by a generation of serfs. How I need I AM to reduce the strength of this city to rubble so I can be free.

During this time of demolition development I thought I was free a couple of times, but either my taskmaster lied or just added links to my bondage chain. His lie was but a brief reprieve from my sin; however, it was extending my slave-chain that was most demoralizing. By lengthening my tether, it allowed me freedom's exhilaration, by walking further in freedom than I had ever gone, only to then be jerked back into the reality my chain still remained. With that quick and sudden tug, my exhilaration was yanked back into hopelessness, even after all of I AM's signs.

But then the light came! The darkness that is my sin, a darkness that can nearly be felt, had no power against the Light. I AM showed me that while darkness covers this world, He is the light that chases the darkness away. Darkness can be in everyone's dwelling, but it doesn't have to be in mine. I understand it now; after tearing down idol after idol with all its ups and downs in the process, I certainly get it. After all of that, my paradigm had shifted, my outlook had changed from constantly looking for my sin to seeking I AM in everything.

Finally it's time to leave this place; finally it's time to make my exodus from this land of bondage, finally it's time to be free.

pause

"...I AM the way, and the truth, and the life...."
John 14:6

Chapter Nine

Only not quite yet; the finality of my deliverance was on hold. I AM wanted me to memorialize this day of freedom even before my exodus. He wanted me to establish this day as the first day of a new year for me; it was to forever be remembered for deliverance even though I was still in slavery. I AM wanted to see my faith.

In my natural man the command was absurd, but I had learned the natural man cannot receive the things of I AM. My spiritual man had seen the personal power of Yahweh. I understood that obedience was better than sacrifice. So I did what He decreed.

I purposed my deliverance in my heart simply because I AM said it to be true. After years of slavery and months of His powerful demonstrations, I am going to be free—all because of Him. I ate of the sacrificed lamb given for me; I applied its blood to my dwelling just as I AM said. I ate it with my eyes fixed on leaving my bondage behind and my feet ready to walk, in freedom, ahead. And in that willingness, in that obedience, I waited. I waited with an anticipation, I waited with reverence, I waited behind the sacrificial blood.

In my pause and in His power, I bowed low and worshiped for I AM was going to both pass through, and pass over, so I could be set free.

Chapter Ten

The midnight cries of death and despair reached deep down in my spirit and they pulled to the surface those experiences in my life. It was only grace that had kept them from being completely fulfilled.

I had killed in the exuberance of my youth. With the sword of my tongue, the spear of my spirit, and the bow of my actions, there were causalities in my past. In fact, that was my initial excuse for running into the wilderness. I was afraid of the truth and hid in the sands of sin. Each passing season dulled the desire to return to reality.

But then came that day of fire.

In an instant I was no longer afraid to return; I was no longer a slave to my fear. I was ready to return and face the taskmaster. My journey was set and I started out…only to experience fear again. But this fear was different.

I was so ill and my son so close to death, all because I had failed to keep I AM's words. It had brought our freedom journey to an abrupt halt, and could have stopped it completely, if it wasn't for intercession. In that intercession I learned some valuable lessons.

First and foremost I learned true fear. I wasn't to fear the truth, but I was to reverence Truth—I wasn't to be afraid of what man could do to my body; rather, I was to reverence the One who had my soul in His hand.

I learned that my deliverance was so much bigger than myself. Without doubt, I AM was needed most, but that did not negate my need for others, those who would intercede and come along my side in this journey.

I learned the depths of my sin; I saw in the near-death of my son how my actions affected those coming up behind me. I saw the need to break my family's bondage.

And I learned the truth to live the truth, to practice all of I AM's words. For His words offer life, an abundant life free from bondage.

As I stood behind the sacrificial lamb's blood, poised to leave this bondage, the cries of sin's wages echoing throughout the land, my taskmaster cried as well. He was ready to let me go, He was done fighting this battle for me. The strength of I AM prevailed as my taskmaster said, "Go, worship the Lord as you have said you would do."

So I left, with hands held high and hope lifted higher, I journeyed out of slavery. My chains were broken and my spirit lifted!! The years of hope had finally become a reality. I was free…only not quite yet. I quickly sensed my departure from bondage only began a new venture into a different wilderness. It was a wilderness where Yahweh would be my only sustainer; and the chief taskmaster would still be around.

parting

"Even from eternity, I AM He…
I act and who can reverse it?"
Isaiah 43:13

Chapter Eleven

Heretofor, taskmaster was first and I AM second in my ageless adolescence, but Yahweh was going to reorder my life. He was going to be first; He was going to show me what it meant for Him to be my Alpha and my Omega.

It was then I also realized how, over these past several months, I AM was more on my mind than my slavery. Yes, I was still in the land of bondage, but my focus wasn't on the land as much as it was on I AM's power in getting me out. My focal point was on Him and His desire to tear down those idols in me. However, to tear them down was not enough, something must be built in their place. Without a rebuild, without allowing I AM to be the replacement, the chief taskmaster would bring back my personal idols some seven times stronger.

I had witnessed I AM's offensive power as He methodically confronted my graven images until each had been torn down. Now however, I was going to experience His defensive power; I was going to see what it was like to have I AM as my fortress and my shield. I was going to experience I AM as the sole God of my life, where He is both my protector and provider. It is a new journey on my road to freedom and one I am ready for.

I think.

Chapter Twelve

I was prepared to do battle along this new journey. I was armed and ready to fight. Yet, we didn't go the way of hostility. There was no first campaign to reminisce, not even a skirmish for practice. There was nothing, and I didn't understand. How could I experience all of I AM's power, have it at the ready, only to surrender it through travel? For I AM led me the long way around rather than straight through a stronghold of my enemy. I was ready to war, only I was entrenched in the wrong conflict.

This first battle was not with my enemy, but with myself. It was to be fought without weapons and spectacular power encounters; rather, it was waged through surrender. I would surrender my will, what I thought was the way and the combat, to I AM's. In that submission I was to learn His ways are higher than mine; that I AM always has what's best for me in His plans; and that His plan always has a purpose that reaches beyond the present. There would be a battle and I AM had the perfect location for me to fight.

He would lead me there, both day and night, by the pillar of His presence. To the natural eye the location was a strategic death plot—just one way in, tucked away with mountains on one side and the sea on the other. The only way in was also the only way out. But it was where I AM wanted me to be.

So I camped in this wilderness retreat, learning to submit in my spirit, and covered by His constant presence. The sight of which, so spiritually perfect, kept my competing flesh at ease, even as I settled down in the place I would never choose to garrison.

Chapter Thirteen

My flesh looked past His presence as the chief taskmaster and his minions thundered towards me. My mind jumbled with thoughts, each one renewed and empowered as the billowing cloud, caused by the rumbling adversary, advanced with military might.

'You should know you can never leave me,' taskmaster's historic voice returned as the sounds of chariot wheels and horse's hooves raced to recapture me. 'You have made an exodus before; yet, you still were a slave,' he reminded me.

I was amazed at my double-mindedness. There, standing by the pillar of presence and perched in I AM's shadow, my flesh responded to antiquity and began to wrestle with my spirit.

'Why not simply die as a slave rather than die trying *not* to be one,' my flesh reasoned. 'At least there was pleasure in that season, unlike the dread you fear now.'

There was a fear…and a dread…and a disappointment at where I stood. I had thought this time was different, this time I really am going to be free. But it wasn't any different. I only wandered briefly around to be backed up in a death bight; and in this place I realized my end was near.

My flesh fed off its carnality and rebelled even stronger as it shifted from accusation to acceptance. 'I wish I never would have left; I should have stayed in bondage and lived...Oh, to never have prayed to leave just to die in this wilderness' was the summation as my heartache burst into heartbreak.

I thought it impossible for my horror to increase, but it did as the taskmaster and his army closed in. I closed my eyes and ears thinking a natural silence would ease my fear. In that closing I hoped to rekindle the innate stillness of my past life, for in that quiet I could escape into the comfort of my bondage.

But my natural blackout was breeched by the piercing light of I AM's voice. He spoke both strong and soft to my spirit, and directed it at the core of my being: "Do not fear."

There with my back to the sea of nowhere and facing the certainty of my adversary, I AM's voice refocused my sight to His presence. The huge pillar that had never left, but one that I had put away, was again before me. It was where I should have kept it all along, in the very center of my sight.

And His presence was on the move.

Chapter Fourteen

Preparing to station Himself both before and behind me—as only He could—I AM authored further instructions to my spirit: "Fear not, sta...," but all that He ordered became a dull hum after His "fear not."

Fear was still my battleground. Hemmed in and with certain death approaching, something I had never thought possible suddenly become a real consideration. What was now before me was of greater dread then living bondage's past: I was going to die in my effort to live. My flesh, in a torturous attempt to return, tried to reignite my terror I AM had just extinguished moments ago.

But, as my flesh wavered in looking at the present, my spirit recalled a benchmark in my past. It was when the flies buzzed the eyes of the world, but mine were left alone. I AM, through that plague, had taught me not to look as the world looked or see what the world sees. His ways are different; His ways are so very much different they cannot be recognized with the natural eye. So as my flesh looked out, my spirit gazed up.

In that upward gaze I saw the eternity of I AM; I saw the strength of everlasting and the majesty of His glory. Then I remembered another lesson from that same benchmark: just whom to fear. I was not to fear those who kill the body, but the One who has my body and soul in His hand. It was one thing to learn the principle; yet, something totally different to live it.

And then it hit me, the revelation that would be the foundation for my life from that time forward. My flesh had tried to skew the truth by using its natural eye when it said I was going to die in my effort to live. But the truth is I must die in order to live. Not a natural death, but a spiritual one. I am to die to myself in order for I AM to live in me.

In that revelation, the commands of I AM previously drowned in that dull hum of fear, returned clarion clear: Fear not, stand still, and see the salvation of the LORD.

There was my answer in how to die to myself. I was to stand still; I was to make no effort on my own other than obey what I AM said. In my obedience I had traveled at the voice of I AM; and now, I AM had brought me to this stationary place. My effort is obedience; His effort is the work. His work in complete, His work is perfect, His work is salvation. It was a work I was going to see by experience.

Chapter Fifteen

"Hold your peace," I AM said in the third watch of the night. It was said at the time of my deliverance's darkest hours, that midnight quarter where the adversary rages in the belly of the night.

Just what does it mean to 'hold my peace' my flesh queried. I AM had already stilled my spirit by addressing my fear; He already shared His desire to fight my battle, and yet, now, I am to hold my peace.

Yes, I AM had given me peace, right here and right now, even within eyesight of the enemy and in a place that seemed conducive to a natural defeat. But He had brought me here; I AM had set the scene in my final act of deliverance. I was to hold on, I was to clutch peace with the death-grip for life. "Hold your peace," I AM had said, and *charash* was the word He used.

Charash I repeated in my being, dragging out both syllables with a hope of understanding. Over and over again I repeated the word: *charash…charash…charash* until, finally, I AM quickened my spirit to its truth. *Charash* means to be silent, to be dumb, to be speechless, to be deaf. While I AM fights; I am *charash*.

I AM needs no exhorting from me, He needs no encouragement for my battle or defensive rationale to justify my fight—I am to be speechless. Not only am I not to speak but I am not to hear either. I am not to listen to all the clamor around me, all the doubts and fears and personal failures that can engulf you in that midnight hour where the adversary whispers. Nothing spoken outward, nothing heard inward, I am *charash*.

In my silence I AM began to move at the breaking of the morning watch, that time when the darkest hours had passed and all things begin to be new. He moved to keep my taskmaster in darkness while, at the same time, shined the light of newness on me. And with the light came the wind—that beautiful wind.

The wind, the *ruach* that had had made man a living soul in the beginning, was blowing on me a new life of freedom. I closed my eyes and breathed in its liberty, savoring the stillness, yet power, of I AM's strength. As I leaned my spirit back to inhale all the breath I possibly could, my eyes caught a glimpse of the impossible happening behind me. The invisible wind in my face was doing a visible work in the rearward.

And I turned about, and I looked, and I couldn't believe what I saw. I AM was doing the impossible and I am going to walk it through.

Chapter Sixteen

"Go forward" was the command in my spirit. But at first there was nowhere to go, in fact, I didn't even know which way was forward. There was only one obvious way out of where I AM had placed me and He was pillared in that way.

But then I felt the wind, I AM's powerful life-giving breath and I turned to see the effect of its blowing. That is the uniqueness of the wind: it can be felt, but not really seen. Yet, you know it's there through its effect, for the results of its blowing makes its invisibility visible.

Then I understood which way forward was in my deliverance. It was two-fold really: it was turning my back to the taskmaster and following the leading breath of I AM. I had spent so much time looking back at my adversary, so much time analyzing, planning, and scheming personal programs for victory that always failed, that I had lost my vision of going forward and leaving my past behind. I had always tried to go forward by looking backward; by walking in reverse I had always fallen.

"Go forward" continued to resonate in my spirit and in my obedience the personally impossible became divinely possible. I AM made a way where there seemed to be no way. The very place He had put me, the confining cove that spoke certain death, had become my way out into life. His breath opened the sea of doubt and defeat that had kept me hemmed in for so many years. I walked through that sea on its once sodden ground for I AM had made it as firm and solid as a rock.

There was no need to look back in fear now, there was no concern for the taskmaster, I was walking on the solid rock. Bolstered by His breath, doubt and defeat were simply walls to my left and right and not the door whose threshold I could never cross.

But I did look back, not in fear, but in authority. Once I passed through the other side of doubt and defeat and stood upright on faith and victory, I AM had me raise my hand in battle. His authority and my obedience was going to defeat—once and for all—this taskmaster in my life.

As my adversary raced to bring me back, attempting to travel the road that had set me free, he failed. Lies and deceit can never prevail when trying to walk on the path of truth. I watch my taskmaster drown in the very water he had used to satisfy my thirsty bondage. The sea he had hoped to be my demise had become his death as his residue washed ashore, totally defeated, on my side of deliverance.

And I was to see this taskmaster no more.

praise

"I AM the Alpha and the Omega…
who is and who was and who is to come,
the Almighty."

Revelation 1:8

Chapter Seventeen

My hand, just moments ago raised in battle, was now lifted up in praise as my spirit burst forth in adulation. Standing on my side of deliverance I sang:

"The Lord is my strength and song, And He has become my salvation; This is my God, and I will praise Him; My father's

God, and I will extol Him. The Lord is a warrior; The Lord is His name."[1]

Yes, the Lord is my warrior, I repeated, surveying the death of my adversary as he lay lifeless on the seashore, as the small waves of doubt and deceit—his weapons--washed over him. Yes, I will see this taskmaster no more, just as I AM said.

My spirit burst forth again in praise: "Who is like You among the gods, O Lord? Who is like You, majestic in holiness, awesome in praises, working wonders? In Your lovingkindness You have led me whom You have redeemed; in Your strength You have guided me to Your holy habitation."

Never in my imagination had I visualized such liberty, never in my wildest dreams had I envisioned such privilege of holiness.

---

[1] Praises selected from Exodus 15.

The fear found in my continued bondage had been drowned in the sea with my adversary. Now my fear was not misplaced as it was for some many years before; now, it was rightfully placed in reverence to the I AM that I AM.

Again I sang to the Lord: "The Lord shall reign forever and ever." It was a chorus that played from my heart over and over again.

Spontaneously I then did something I had never done before. My flesh, that part of me that always listened to the taskmaster was now hearing my praise. Accordingly, it joined in my jubilation finally being in step with my spirit, as I picked up a tambourine and danced before the Lord. Tears of joy flowed from my eyes, praise streamed from my lips, and my feet danced in unprecedented peace as my whole being celebrated before the Lord.

And I sang even more to the Him, for the Lord is highly exalted and He is worthy to be praised; I am finally free by the power of I AM…let us exalt His holy name!

About the Author

Pastor John Pace accepted Christ in 1981 and has spent the past 33 years in full-time ministry. His efforts in serving the Lord in denominational leadership with the Church of God of Prophecy (Cleveland, TN) took him to over 40 states and 40 countries around the world. Still, there is no place he would rather be than in the presence of the Lord and at Crimson House.

As the founding Pastor of Crimson House in 2001, Pastor John transplanted a fledgling local church on the outskirts of town into the heart of historic Springfield. It has now become a lively urban ministry center, with an active local body offering assistance and programs to over 750 non-congregants each month. His anointing to show people the love of Jesus and his laid-back teaching style create a culture of discipleship and belonging. One of his greatest rewards is to hear someone call Crimson House "home."

Pastor John attended Gordon-Conwell Theological Seminary. He enjoys spending time with his wonderful wife, Diane, and their seven beautiful children.

Additional books and resources written by Pastor John can be found at www.readjohnpace.com.